CW01335714

Snowboarding Basics: All About Snowboarding

ISBN-13: 978-1479394500
ISBN-10: 1479394505

SNOWBOARDING BASICS:
ALL ABOUT SNOWBOARDING

Steve Kalley

I dedicate this to the lucky people who've been touched by the fun, excitement and buzz of snowboarding...

Contents

Snowboarding:
A Brief History

No one may be able to tell for sure who the real pioneer of snowboarding is, but some facts about the sport's young history are non-debatable and widely accepted all over the world.

It would definitely be a good idea to learn more about the sport's history and the things that pushed it to its current popularity, especially if you're planning to start learning how to snowboard.

It was in 1929 when M.J. Burchett first glided over snow on a piece of plywood secured to his feet by some clotheslines.

Although some would disagree, many people consider this as the origin of snowboarding.

Another milestone in snowboarding history occurred in 1963, when eighth grade student Tom Sims built something he dubbed "ski board" as a class project.
Just like Burchett's contraption, this was also made from plywood, which was primarily why Sims called it a board.

Two years later, Sherman Poppen introduced the world to the "Snurfer," which was basically a contraption made from two skis bolted together.

The contraption was originally created as a toy for Poppen's children, but he soon started organizing Snurfer competitions.

The 1970s were known as the years when snowboarding was finally able to build a strong base.

The year 1970 saw the surfer Dimitrije Milovich coming up with the idea of creating some sort of surfboard for snow.

In 1975, Newsweek featured Milovich and the board he named Winterstick.

Soon after that, Jake Burton began using fibreglass and steam-bent wood to build his own version of the board.

By the end of the decade, Burton had gone as far as adding steel edges to the sides of the board and bindings that provide better support and added control.

In 1980, the development of snowboarding was unwittingly hastened by skiing, as it gave Burton and the Winterstick manufacturers the idea to use a P-Tex base on their boards.

By 1982, people finally saw the very first international snowboarding competition, which was held in Vermont.

The venue was a run called "The Face."

The mid-1980s had the snowboarding community facing difficulties, considering that only 39 of the over 600 ski resorts allowed snowboards on their slopes.

This gave the snowboarders a very limited range of options as regards where they can practice the sport.

Things changed abruptly in 1997, when the ban against snowboards came to a sudden halt.

It seemed that people grew to accept the sport overnight and liked it almost as much as they did skiing.

Today, snowboarding has grown so much and still continues to grow such that the number of skiers in the United States alone is said to have dropped by 25 percent.

In contrast, the number of snowboarders rose by 77 percent, thus making it today's fastest growing sport.

About twenty percent of those who visit ski resorts in the United States these days are snowboarders.

And if you've been to any of these resorts lately, then you may have noticed that more people are taking interest in snowboarding.

It has even been projected that by the year 2015, more people will be snowboarding than skiing.

Popularity of Snowboarding

If you happen to spend your winter vacation in any of the popular ski resorts anywhere in the world, then you'll likely notice that the slopes are dotted with snowboards.

There are even those who say that snowboards will soon surpass skis in terms of popularity.

Since time immemorial, people have always enjoyed sliding and gliding down snow-covered slopes.

This may be why it's a bit difficult to say for sure who invented the very first snowboard.

In places where snow was a seasonal or normal occurrence, evidence has been found of ancient civilizations snowboarding with the use of crude contraptions.

In Hawaii, for example, there are mountaintops typically blanketed with snow every winter.

It has been discovered that ancient Hawaiians had a pastime that involved gliding on snow using "ti leaf sleds" and that this pastime is still being practiced even today.

There is even an annual snowboarding competition held on the island every winter.

Gliding on snow from 9,000 feet above sea level with an ocean view below can indeed be an amazing experience.

Two of the people credited for the development of snowboarding are Jack Burchette, who created a plywood plank contraption in 1929 and Sherman Poppen, who created a special sled for his children in 1965.

Regardless of who invented the snowboard first, though, it has indeed gone through a remarkable evolution.

Today, snowboards have become an integral part of people's ski vacations.

When you see the number of snowboarders sliding down the slopes these days, it's difficult to believe there was once a time when snowboards were banned on the slopes of many ski resorts.

That was the time when they were considered nuisances. But now, snowboarding is a legitimate sport with a lot of followers worldwide.

The very first major manufacturer of snowboards is Avalanche Snowboards, which was established in 1982.

Needless to say, it became the forerunner to several other manufacturers that soon came onto the scene.

What sets Avalanche apart is that they're still the only snowboard manufacturer that offers lifetime warranties on their boards to this day.

The same year that Avalanche was established, Vermont hosted the very first national snowboarding competition in the United States. This was the very first time riders from different parts of the country could test their skills against each other.

In 1985, the very first magazine dedicated to snowboarding was published.

It was originally called Absolutely Radical, but the name was changed six months later to International Snowboard Magazine.

Just as Vermont hosted the first U.S. National Championships, it also opened the very first snowboarding park in the country.

In 1989, the ban on snowboards was lifted in most ski resorts, as resort owners finally acknowledged the growing popularity of the sport and succumbed to the demands of the public.

Snowboarding then became a legitimate sport worldwide when it was included in the 1998 Winter Olympics.

In its relatively short history spanning 40 years, snowboarding has indeed won the hearts of many people all over the world.

Basic Snowboarding Equipment

So, you're planning a grand winter vacation.

You may already have booked tickets to Europe or anywhere in the United States.

And you're probably looking forward to looking out your cabin window and enjoying a lovely scene amidst a snowy backdrop.

But, if you're not satisfied with simply looking out at a lovely scene and you want to bring the excitement of your winter adventure up a notch, then why don't you try some fast-paced fun?

Get on a snowboard and hit those snowy slopes!

You'll surely be glad you did as you experience an entirely different world.

Of course, you need to take a few things into consideration before you go snowboarding for the first time.

Among those things are the essential pieces of equipment you may want to buy for yourself or rent at the resort you're visiting.

Obviously, the very first thing you need is a good snowboard.

It would be pointless to go snowboarding without a board, right?

You may as well just stand in the snow and make snowballs. When you look at snowboards, you might mistakenly think all boards are the same and that it's a one-size-fits-all contraption.

That isn't actually the case.

The snowboard you use should match your skill level, your riding style, your size or weight, and the conditions under which you'll be riding.

Considering all these factors, the task of choosing a snowboard for yourself can indeed be tricky, especially when you're a beginner in the sport.

It's therefore important to do some research when shopping for a board of your own.

Another important thing you need when you go snowboarding is a good pair of boots.

It's not advisable for you to simply get on a snowboard in a regular pair of footwear.
There are boots designed specifically for clicking into a snowboard's bindings.

This helps ensure that you're secure and practically glued down to your board.

They offer adequate support and help ensure you can focus all of your energy on the board itself.

Furthermore, these specially-designed boots also help ensure that your feet are kept warm in the cold winter conditions.

Like the snowboard itself, you have to make sure the boots you choose suits you well. You may want to get boots with heat moulding liners and gel padding.

Other than the board and a pair of boots, you'll also need bindings for snowboarding. The bindings are fitted to your board and designed such that your boots can click into place.

Screws are used to attach the bindings to the snowboard. These screws help ensure the bindings are sturdy enough and that they'll hold you in place as you slide down the slopes.

And now that you know what the three basic pieces of equipment needed for snowboarding are, you should be ready to start hitting the slopes and learning the basic snowboarding skills.

Pretty soon, you may even start practicing some snowboarding tricks and participating in local snowboarding competitions. So, grab a board now and have some fun!

Bindings

So, you've finally bought a snowboard and are excited to use it on your next winter vacation.

What's next?

Well, you'll have to find the right bindings, of course! Now, you may wonder just how important bindings are for snowboarding.

You need to realise that these are essential for your safety as you glide down those slopes. The bindings allow you to make sure your boots are held secure against the board.

Remember as well that different people have different riding styles and will therefore need different types of bindings.

Naturally, you'll have to choose the type of bindings best suited to your riding style as well as your sense of fashion. Here are the five types of bindings you can choose from:

1. Strap Bindings

This type of bindings is comprised of three parts: the base plate, the straps, and the high-back plate.

The base plate catches the boots and has a contoured shape. The straps hold your ankles and the front of your feet; they're found at the front of the bindings.

The high-back plate rises in a perpendicular manner from the base and secures your heels as well as the back of your lower legs. When you use this type of bindings, the only way you can get off the snowboard is to manually release the straps.

2. Step-in Bindings

This type of bindings is comprised of three parts: the base plate, the step-in mechanism, and the back plate. It is deemed more convenient because it allows you to just step onto the board and automatically latch into it. The problem is that they lack functionality, provide much less control, and offer much less support. They do provide you with an extra kick in terms of speed. Needless to say, you need to choose step-in boots as well if you choose this type of bindings.

3. Flow-in Bindings

This type of bindings is comprised of three parts: the base plate, the tongue, and the back plate lever.

It employs a reclining mechanism, which allows you to unlock and recline the back of the bindings so your feet can enter easily. It offers the control you get from strap bindings as well as the ease you get from step-in bindings. The drawback is that this type of bindings is much more difficult to adjust than strap bindings.

4. Plate Bindings

This type of bindings is comprised of three parts: the base plate, the lever, and the steel bails. It combines hard boots and stiffer bindings that give you more control over your snowboard. It also allows for snow carving and high-speed riding.

5. Baseless Bindings

This type of bindings should be used only by those who've already mastered the sport of snowboarding. As indicated by the name, this type of bindings doesn't have a base. Your boots will therefore be in direct contact with your snowboard. The drawback to this is the difficulty in adjusting as well as the 'toe drag' caused to riders with big feet.

It may be a good idea to buy your boots at the same time you buy your bindings so you can be sure they fit well together.

Whatever bindings you choose, be sure to practice getting into and out of them before hitting the slopes.

Apparel

A huge part of the appeal of snowboarding lies in the fact that it allows you to participate in an activity held at some of the world's most beautiful landscapes.

Take note, though, that spending an extended period of time on snowy slopes exposes you to potentially harmful climates.

This makes it extremely important for you to ensure you're wearing the right clothing when you head out to the slopes.

Your clothes should keep you warm, comfortable, and protected at all times so you can enjoy snowboarding even more.

The clothes you wear should also be lightweight and should have the ability to keep you dry.

The best way to ensure protection and comfort during a snowboarding adventure is to use three layers of clothing.

This enables you to adjust to sudden temperature changes by removing or adding layers accordingly.

In fact, most winter sports require this three-layer system of getting dressed. The base layer is meant to trap warmth and keep moisture away from you.

The middle layer is meant to provide added insulation. The outer layer is meant to serve as protection against rain and harsh winds.

Following is a brief guide on the importance of each layer and what it should consist of.

Base Layer

This layer should completely cover you. It should therefore include thermal underwear, a long-sleeved thermal shirt, a pair of full-length leggings, and snowboarding socks.

The best material for these pieces of clothing is polypropylene or any material that can effectively wick moisture from your skin.

As mentioned above, this layer is meant to keep you warm and dry. If you have a low tolerance for itchiness, then you should stay away from materials that contain wool.

Middle Layer

This layer should consist of a jacket or sweater, a pair of snowboarding pants, and a pair of snowboarding boots. The most commonly used materials for this layer being wool and fleece.

Fleece is especially preferable because of its lightweight and breathable properties. On warmer days, this layer can serve as the outer layer of your clothing. It's a good idea to choose pants with a roomy fit and padding in the backside and knee areas for protection against impact.

Outer Layer

This layer should consist of a hat, beanie, or helmet. Whichever of the three you choose, you have to be sure that it covers your ears. You will also need snowboarding goggles, a snowboarding jacket, and snowboarding gloves.

In choosing snowboarding goggles, make sure the lenses have scratch-resistant and anti-fog coating as well as a hundred percent UV protection.

Finally, your jacket and gloves should be water-resistant.

When you go out to shop for snowboarding apparel, you have to make sure it fits well so you can prevent chafing and maximize the breathable properties of the clothes.

The right clothing serves to keep you warm, comfortable, and safe as you slide down those slopes on your snowboard.

Therefore, it's definitely worth your time and money to make sure you get the best snowboarding apparel you can find.

Types of Snowboarding

When you hear people talk about snowboarding, perhaps your first thought is for people going downhill at amazing speeds.

And when you watch people participating in the sport, it may look very simple and easy to do.

But, the truth is that snowboarding is a pretty complex sport and quite difficult to master.

Furthermore, the sport doesn't just come in a single form.

There are actually four main varieties of snowboarding, namely: freestyle, freeriding, freecarve, and jibbing.

Freestyle typically involves displaying snowboarding tricks as well as impressive speed.

Professional snowboarders can truly show off their snowboarding skill in this event, which gives them the freedom to execute jumps and other tricks whenever they want.

A more flexible type of snowboard is used for this snowboarding style. This board enables them to jump much higher than they'd normally be able to on a regular snowboard.

The most common snowboarding style if freeriding and this is perhaps the style that immediately comes to mind whenever you hear the word 'snowboarding'.

This is the style that's most advisable for beginners to learn before moving on to other snowboarding styles.

It typically involves going down the slopes diagonally. Your aim when snowboarding in this style is to get from one side of the slope to the other.

Freecarve is a snowboarding race participated in by two professional snowboarders. The race involves the use of all techniques and skills they may have mastered.

These skills and techniques include twisting, turning, balancing, and shifting their weight as needed.

The aim of a participant in this kind of race is to pass his opponent at a specific point where they're required to use a particular skill or a combination of skills to ensure a safe passage.

Jibbing refers to someone who uses his snowboard on a surface that's not snow.

When you watch advanced snowboarders do their thing on the slopes, you'll likely see them performing tricks on rails, benches, and ledges, among other things.

It is when they use these surfaces that they're said to be jibbing. As a spectator, you may find these tricks a lot of fun to behold.

But, you should bear in mind that a lot of accidents have occurred as a result of jibbing. This makes it important for you to make sure you've truly reached advanced levels in your snowboarding skills before you try this style.

Snowboarding can definitely be exciting and interesting to watch whether on an actual slope or on TV.

But, it can be even more exciting if you start learning how to do it yourself.

It can be a bit difficult to imagine that this sport gained popularity only about 40 years ago, considering the speed with which its popularity is increasing in this day and age.

Taking part in the sport is an entirely different matter from watching it and cheering for your favourite participants.

The very first time you slide down those slopes on a snowboard, you'll surely discover a whole new world of fun and excitement.

Where to Go Snowboarding

Snowboarding has indeed gained massive popularity in recent years. If you're one of those people who want to learn this exciting sport, then you need to be prepared for a whole lot of challenge.

This is one sport that requires a high level of skill and can be difficult to master. But, once you do master it, it can easily become an integral part of your life and may even become the primary reason for you to travel to places you never thought you'd ever set foot on.

You'll probably start spending your holidays in place where you can enjoy the sport while discovering the world's most scenic spots.

In the past, skiing was considered the primary winter sport. In fact, when snowboarding was first developed and when it was just starting to gain some popularity, a majority of winter vacation spots prohibited the use of snowboards on their slopes.

These days, however, things have changed completely and an estimated 97 percent of ski resorts and winter vacation spots have opened their slopes to snowboarders and skiers alike.

If you're just starting to search for a good place to practice your snowboarding skills, therefore, then you're lucky enough to have a wide range of choices, unlike people in the past whose choice of slopes were extremely limited.

Many snowboarding enthusiasts agree that Tignes in France is among the best places to practice the sport. France is noted to have the longest snowboarding season in Europe.

And people who've visited this snowboarding location once usually come back for more, especially since it gives them the opportunity to visit new slopes they haven't been to before.

Once you've gained enough confidence in your snowboarding skills, you may even go down one or more of the off-piste slopes that can be found in the area.

As a beginner, though, you'd do well to spend your time on the motorway runs. Other than excellent slopes for daytime adventures, the area is also said to offer a great nightlife.

But, what people love most about the place is their relaxed attitude as regards dress codes.

If you wish to snowboard in the United States, then you may want to visit Utah, which is said to have the best snowboarding locations.

The Canyons Resort has sealed its place in history by being the first resort to open its slopes to snowboarding.

Another resort in the area that's part of the sport's history is Park City Mountain Resort, which was where the 2002 Winter Olympics were held.

The average snowfall in the area is 360 inches, so you'll never have any problems associated with a lack of snow, that's for sure.

Wherever you decide to spend your winter adventure and no matter which slopes you choose to snowboard on, you'll surely enjoy yourself.

Being able to spend a relaxing time away from the stresses of work, while getting to experience a sport as exhilarating as snowboarding is surely the best kind of vacation ever.

The holiday adventure you'll have will definitely be one you aren't likely to forget for as long as you live.

Learning the Basics

Watching people sliding down mountain slopes on snowboards can be quite fascinating, especially when they do it with so much ease.

When you try the sport for the first time, however, you're likely to discover that it's not nearly as easy as it seems.

You may have bought the best snowboarding equipment and accessories you can find, but your first downhill ride will still involve some difficulty.

One thing that would make things easier is learning the basics on your first snowboarding session from an expert.

It would also help if you brought along some basic knowledge in the first place.

One of the first things you should ensure before going out on the slopes is that you have the right snowboard.

This means your board shouldn't be too long or too short. It should also have just the right width for your skill level.

Riding the wrong board will definitely make your first ride even more difficult than would normally be.

When you go out to shop for a snowboard, you may take advice from the sales representative as regards the right choice or bring along a friend with considerable snowboarding experience to help you find the right board.

It's equally important for you to understand that snowboarding and skiing are entirely different things.

Perhaps their only similarity is that they both have you going downhill at amazing speeds.

So, even if you're an experienced skier, that shouldn't mean you can just take the basics of snowboarding for granted.

Many people have gotten into trouble on the slopes due to overconfidence regarding their skills.

The good thing about having skiing experience is that it helps you learn the snowboarding basics a lot more quickly.

You should always strive to keep yourself relaxed as you get on your board for the very first time.

You should also keep your knees slightly bent so as to avoid getting hurt in case you stumble and fall.

As soon as you get comfortable on the board, try moving your feet one at a time, making small movements to start with.

The next step is for you to try moving forward, but not going downhill yet.

It's important to try sliding across the hill first so as to ensure safety even in the case of a fall. Once you get comfortable with the sliding motion, that's the time to try going downhill.

Bear in mind the basic rules of snowboarding.

For example, you need to steer with your front foot at all times. If you wish to execute a toe-side turn, then you need to lift your heel and then push your toe down.

In the same way, a heel-side turn is executed by lifting your toe and then pushing down your heel.

If you wish to stop, then you need to turn your feet in such manner that your downhill progress slows down and eventually stops.

As you start learning the basics of the sport, you should also start learning about safety and protection.

Among other things, you need to make sure you're wearing the appropriate snowboarding gear to make sure your snowboarding experience is kept injury-free.

Tips and Tricks for Beginners

As a beginner in snowboarding, it's important for you to take some advice from more experienced snowboarders before you start learning even the most basic snowboarding tricks.

This helps you make sure that your first snowboarding adventure is a safe and truly enjoyable one.

Following are a few basic suggestions you'd do well to bear in mind if you want to have a truly amazing snowboarding experience.

Your number one concern when you decide to get into the sport of snowboarding should be your own health.

In fact, this consideration should be foremost on your mind before you even step onto the slopes.

You could limber up by taking daily walks, which can also help strengthen your lungs.

Take note that the amount of effort you need to exert with every movement is one of the most obvious clues to your fitness level.

By that you can tell whether you're in good physical shape or not.

It's also important to understand the value of having the right snowboarding gear.

This can spell the difference between an amazing and a horrendous snowboarding experience.

If your snowboarding boots are an excellent fit, then they'll surely be able to improve your balance, thus allowing you to enjoy your ride even more.

You'd also do well to wear a helmet of top quality.

After all, looking good on the slopes and getting the exhilarating feeling of the cool wind on your face wouldn't really do much for you if you end up at the hospital after a fall.

As soon as you've adequately prepared yourself for your snowboarding adventure, it's time to learn a few basic tricks.

Among the best tricks for a beginner to learn and what's normally being used as a warm-up trick by experts are grabs.

The first grab trick you may want to try is the indie, which involves grabbing the toe-side edge of your board with your back hand.

You may also want to try the mute, wherein you grab the toe-side edge with your front hand.

The melon is a trick that has you grabbing the heel-side edge with your front hand. With the stale-fish, you grab the heel-side edge with your back hand.

The tail is where you catch the board's tail end using your back hand. Conversely, the nose is where you grab the snowboard's nose end with your front hand.

Finally, you could try executing the method, which is similar to the melon, except that you pull your snowboard upwards and then stick out your hind leg.

Perhaps the most important thing to remember is that you shouldn't try to do too much at once. Take things slow and be patient in learning how to snowboard.

Taking things too fast will only serve to demolish your own confidence in your abilities.

As long as you keep the above tips in mind and work patiently on mastering these basic tricks, you should have a fun and fulfilling snowboarding experience.

The best thing is that you can work on becoming a better snowboarder each time you step onto the slopes.

Developing Muscle Memory

You may not have realised this, but one of the most vital aspects of doing well in any sport is developing muscle memory.

Therefore, if you're learning how to snowboard, it's important for you to learn how you can train your muscles accordingly.

Perhaps the first thing you need to understand is the nature of muscle memory. This can be defined simply as your muscles' natural ability to remember a set of movements.

For example, whenever someone throws a ball at you, you're able to catch it automatically because of muscle memory.

You therefore need to develop muscle memory for snowboarding in order for the manoeuvres to become second nature to you.

Whenever you go out on the slopes on your snowboard and execute a 360 spin, you're practically asking your muscles to search their memory banks for the series of movements that'll allow you to properly execute the spin.

Now, what makes this so important and why is it necessary for your muscles to recall every single movement you learn, anyway?

Well, the better muscle memory you have, the more you can expect to perfectly land your snowboarding tricks.

Here's how to develop muscle memory for snowboarding:

1. Technique

Before you work on muscle memory, you need to learn the proper technique first. It would do you no good to let your muscles recall the wrong movements. If there's anything wrong with your technique, you should fix it immediately.

Remember that the longer you wait to correct a mistake, the more difficult it will be to retrain your muscle memory.

You certainly don't want the wrong technique to become part of your muscle memory, do you?

2. Visualization

In order to make sure you execute the right technique, it would be best to go through the movements in your mind before you actually execute it.

It's crucial for you to learn how to view every single action in your mind if you want to make your muscles perform the movements correctly. Mental practice is the necessary first step towards effective physical training.

3. Repetition

Muscle memory isn't developed in an instant. You need to give your muscles enough time to recall all of the movements for every trick.

In the same way you learned how to walk one step at a time, your muscles also need to learn snowboarding movements one step at a time.

This is why you need to keep repeating each technique until your muscles remember every movement it entails.

4. Routine

Develop your own snowboarding routine, which leads up to a specific manoeuvre. This means you need to go from visualizing to executing a particular technique in the same way every single time. Doing things exactly the same way with each repetition allows you to develop muscle memory much more quickly.

Just like with almost everything else, practice is what will bring you to perfect execution of your snowboarding tricks.

As long as you stick to your regular practice routines, you should be able to develop muscle memory soon enough.

And then snowboarding will be even more exciting than ever!

Improving Your Progression

Naturally, all snowboarding enthusiasts want to improve their skills.

But, why do some people seem to progress a lot more quickly than others?

You've been practicing endlessly and doing your best to learn the various snowboarding tricks, but why are things still going so slow for you?

Well, you may want to take heed of the following tips on how to advance more quickly in snowboarding:

1. Avoid trying to accomplish too much at once. This means you shouldn't veer too far away from your comfort zone when trying new tricks. While it's indeed advisable for you to step beyond your comfort zone in order to improve your skills, that doesn't mean you have to go all out on your first try.

   For example, when you've become very comfortable on the intermediate ski run, it may be time to try the basic expert ski run. What you shouldn't do is jump right onto an advanced expert ski run!

Remember that falling and getting a few bruises are part of the learning process, but ending up at the hospital definitely is not!

2. Take time to learn the proper method or technique for whatever snowboarding trick you want to pull off. Practicing with the wrong technique not only hampers your progress, but also contributes to bad habits that'll be very difficult to remove in the future.

   On the other hand, adopting the right technique for every snowboarding trick you're trying to learn will surely make the learning process go a lot more smoothly and move at a quicker pace.

3. Learn snowboarding with a friend who can help you improve your skills.

   Whenever you snowboard with someone whose skills are more advanced than yours, you'll notice that you become more motivated to try new tricks that you would otherwise be too afraid to try.

4. A more experienced friend can also be a source for helpful snowboarding tips and valuable advice.

5. Take lessons. Though you may be able to learn the basics of snowboarding from a friend who's been into the sport for some time, you'll still benefit a lot from as little as a week of snowboarding classes.

   Excellent snowboarding instructors won't only teach you the fundamentals of the sport, but they'll also help you fix any mistake in your snowboarding technique.

6. Record your snowboarding adventures on video. This allows you to review your riding technique and see if there are any mistakes you need to fix. This simple practice can make a world of difference to your future performances.

As an added tip, you may also want to check out snowboarding videos on the internet to see what good technique looks like.

You may then compare this to your own video so you can fix what needs to be fixed and improve on your overall snowboarding performance.

As long as you bear these tips in mind and apply them the next time you go out on the slopes, you'll surely see the progression of your skills move a lot more quickly than before.

Snowboarding in
Deep Powder

Days when there's deep powder are among the most fun-filled days out on the snow.

However, snowboarding in deep powder requires the use of certain strategies and techniques.

Here are some of the techniques you can use when you go deep powder snowboarding:

1. Use only light pressure when you turn in deep powder, except when you're aiming for a tight turn. When you turn too hard, you'll likely create an angle with excessive edge.

   This means your snowboard is likely to burrow into the powder, thus having you end up in about 30cm of snow. A light touch, on the other hand, helps keep you on top of the powder.

2. The most common mistake beginners make when snowboarding in powder, particularly when they turn, is leaning over the board's nose and using the upper body in executing the turn.

This will only serve to dig your board's nose deep into the snow and have you flying high into the air. You wouldn't want that to happen, would you?

What you need to do instead is try to focus your weight in the centre of your board or a little towards the back.

When you turn, you should do so using your ankles, knees, and hips rather than your upper body. If you've ever gone surfing before, then you should already have an idea of how it feels to snowboard in deep powder.

3. Speed is your friend. Take note that powder has a tendency for slowing down your board, so you should do your best to keep the speed up. Speed helps you avoid getting bogged down when snowboarding on flat runs.

Now, what if you're snowboarding on a gladed run?

This is a lot more difficult than snowboarding on a flat run. In fact, this is believed to be among the most difficult snowboarding skills to learn.

Therefore, you shouldn't be discouraged if you fall and somehow get swamped. Here are a few tips for snowboarding in deep snow on gladed runs:

1. Take note that your body always follows the direction of your head. Therefore, when you turn your head towards the trees, then you'll likely end up smack against a tree. This makes it very important for you to always turn your head towards the gap between the trees.

2. Unless you know the area by heart, you should refrain from going fast down a gladed run. Familiarise the run by going down at a slower pace first. You may then increase your pace as the area becomes more and more familiar to you.

3. The combination of a rapid pace, sharp turns in powder, and an obstacle course is what makes gladed runs extremely difficult to master. It's a good idea to plan your turns ahead whenever you're snowboarding down a gladed run.

4. The closer together the trees are, the more important it is for you to know where best you can execute a turn. This helps you avoid running into any of the trees.

5. Bear in mind that gladed runs tend to have a number of tree wells, or deep snow chambers at the base of the trees. These areas can be very dangerous when you get stuck in them, considering the possibility of more snow dropping from the branches of the tree and covering your face.

6. As much as possible, snowboard in gladed runs with a friend and always keep within sight of each other.

Snowboarding Like a Pro

The excitement and exhilaration you get from snowboarding can be both powerful and liberating.

The good news is that there are a number of ways for you to enjoy the sport even more.

There are a number of practice areas you'd do well to explore if you want to improve your snowboard ride.

1. Mental Training

Snowboarding requires courage, but definitely not recklessness. Developing the courage and confidence to improve you snowboarding skills requires some effective mental strategies. You can take your cue from sports psychology for this purpose.

2. Fitness

Snowboarding may look easy from the viewpoint of a spectator, but it's a gruelling sport that requires fitness in order to deliver the best performance.

Your abdominal and leg muscles will naturally be used heavily when you snowboard, which is why you need regular strength training to achieve the fitness level required for the sport. Crunches, squats, hamstring curls, and dead lifts are among the best exercises you can do to target the muscle groups most commonly used in snowboarding.

3. Agility

You may think snowboarding involves nothing more than going down the slopes while balancing on a board, but it actually involves navigating the board as well, which is why you definitely need to develop your agility.

Turning and stopping on tight trails can be very difficult without adequate agility. And how can you ever hope to accomplish those amazing snowboarding jumps and tricks if you're not agile enough? Agility is definitely something you need to develop if you truly want to snowboard like a pro.

4. Impact Protection

Needless to say, you'll likely experience a lot of bumps and falls as you practice the different snowboarding skills.

This makes it important to protect yourself from impact. Remember that you want to learn a sport without killing or maiming yourself in the process. There's nothing exciting about rolling down the slope instead of sliding without a helmet or any protective gear.

In the same way, it's no fun running into a tree when you're unprotected. You could end up at the hospital with broken bones and needing screws installed to get fractures fixed.

What's worse is when your bones refuse to break cleanly and quietly, and choose to pierce your skin instead to display your recklessness to the world. There's really nothing glamorous about that, is there?

It can be easy to feel invincible the first time you successfully snowboard down the slopes. This is especially true of those who've managed to go snowboarding a couple of times without getting into an accident.

Be careful not to become overconfident and always bear in mind that no one is invincible. Even when you aren't practicing new tricks, it's still advisable to wear protective gear whenever you snowboard.

Top-quality helmet, wrist guards, and impact shorts are the most basic items that should be part of your gear.

The above tips should point you in the right direction towards snowboarding like a pro.

Prepare yourself mentally, improve your physical fitness, develop agility, and wear impact protection gear. Most importantly, be safe and enjoy!

Safety Tips

Where snowboarding is concerned, perhaps the most valuable safety tip you need to bear in mind is to always have awareness of your surroundings.

This means before you even step onto your snowboard, you have to look around and observe what other riders are doing and what type of terrain you'll be riding on.

You may think a mountainside is too huge for you to actually run into someone else as you snowboard, but collisions actually happen every day among snowboarders, particularly among beginners.

And the most common reason for these collisions is the snowboarder's failure to observe the things that are going on around him at the time.

Another important safety tip you need to bear in mind is that you have to dress properly for a snowboarding adventure.

It's a given that a snowy mountain will have cold weather, but you never know how cold it'll be or how powdery the snow will be when you get there.

It could even happen that the weather will change and temperatures will suddenly rise or drop while you're already on the slopes.

You wouldn't want to be caught in a blizzard with only a thin sweater on, would you? This is why it's best to dress in layers when you snowboard. You can add or drop layers accordingly as temperatures change.

An avalanche is a common occurrence on mountainsides after a snowstorm.

It's also common for ski patrols to throw dynamites in known avalanche zones so as to prevent skiers and snowboarders from starting one while enjoying their vacation.

However, this doesn't mean the possibility of you starting an avalanche is completely gone.

What do you do if you suddenly find yourself starting to get sucked down the mountain by loose snow?

Well, you should strive to move horizontally across the slope and away from the avalanche zone.

You should then stop and wait for everything to settle before starting downhill again.

If there's no way for you to get away from the avalanche zone in time, then you should do your best to swim with the snow to avoid getting buried in it.

It's always a good idea to start small and then slowly work your way to more advanced snowboarding skills when you feel comfortable enough.

Remember that the most common cause of injury in snowboarding is trying to do things that are way out of your league.

Just because a trick looks easy when someone else does it doesn't mean you can do it without constant and consistent practice. Snowboarding basically requires two things: experience and common sense.

No matter how much training you get in the sport, you aren't likely to get very far in it if you lack common sense.

Bear in mind that most injuries that happen on the slopes happen not because of a lack of training, but because of a lack of common sense.

In everything you do, safety should be your utmost concern and it is your common sense that'll keep you safe on the slopes.

Overcoming Your Fear

Learning the sport of snowboarding is difficult in itself.

It's even more difficult when you're a beginner trying to execute your very first snowboarding tricks.

The difficulty you experience can be both physical and mental.

Of course, this isn't to say you shouldn't try any tricks when you're still a beginner.

In fact, learning how to execute tricks is among the things that make snowboarding interesting and fun!

You just need to remember that you should avoid trying to do any advanced snowboarding trick without first mastering the most basic ones.

More importantly, you need to overcome the fear that commonly hounds beginners if you ever hope to master any snowboarding trick.

The thought of falling and hurting yourself can indeed be daunting, but there are things you can do to handle your fear.

1. Get Lessons

Many of the dry-slopes and resorts open to snowboarding offer lessons as well.

The good thing about these lessons is that they typically involve methods that are taught in accordance with your snowboarding ability. Even better news is that these lessons can be a lot of fun.

Having fun is definitely one of the most effective ways to take your mind off of your fear.

When you're having fun with the other people who are going through the same process as you, you no longer focus on the negative things that could possibly happen if you fail to execute a trick properly.

2. Start Small

Just as you had to learn how to walk one step at a time, you should also develop your snowboarding skills by starting with the basics and then slowly moving forward until you're able to execute more advanced manoeuvres.

If you go directly to jumps and rails, you'll be more likely to fall flat on your face, thus increasing your fear.

But, by mastering ground tricks first, you get to build the confidence you need for conquering the more difficult tricks later on.

3. Get a Buddy

When you try new tricks with a friend or a group of friends, then you get the chance to help each other out.

You'll also have a support system to provide you with encouragement when you encounter difficulties with certain tricks.

Seeing your friends accomplish each trick you're practicing will build your confidence that it can be done and that you, too, can accomplish it in time.

And you have to admit, there's nothing better than a friendly rivalry when it comes to learning a sport while having fun.

Perhaps the most important tip you need to remember is that you should never try to do tricks that are too advanced for your level of skills.

Fear can be a good thing because it keeps you from trying to do things that may be too dangerous.

However, too much fear can also prevent you from reaching your true potential as a snowboarder.

It's therefore extremely important for you to learn how to balance confidence and caution so you can truly enjoy the sport of snowboarding and keep yourself safe while doing so.

Printed in Great Britain
by Amazon.co.uk, Ltd.,
Marston Gate.